IN EVERY S

PITT POETRY SERIES
Ed Ochester, Editor

In Every Seam

ALLISON JOSEPH

University of Pittsburgh Press

Published by the University of Pittsburgh Press,
Pittsburgh, Pa. 15261

Copyright © 1997, Allison Joseph

All rights reserved

Manufactured in the United States of America

Printed on acid-free paper

10 9 8 7 6 5 4 3 2

Library of Congress Cataloging-in-Publication data and acknowledgments are located at the end of this book.

A CIP catalog record for this book is available from the British Library.

The publication of this book is supported by a grant from the Pennsylvania Council on the Arts.

For Jon

CONTENTS

Summers on Screvin — 1

On Sidewalks, on Street Corners, as Girls — 4

Traitor — 6

Urban Games — 9

Malice — 11

Five and Dime — 14

Playing Rough — 17

Arts and Crafts — 20

Barbie's Little Sister — 23

Funny Pages — 25

Fishing — 28

Bribery — 31

Artist-in-Residence — 34

It's Tough to Be a Girl Scout in the City — 37

My Father's Heroes — 40

The Tenant — 43

Day Tripping — 46

Motives — 49

The Swimming Pool — 52

Señora Williams — 56

Life Science   —   59

The Art of Vallejo   —   62

Talking to Marilyn   —   65

Screen Test   —   68

Higher Education   —   71

Academic Instructions   —   74

The First Time   —   77

The White People Next Door   —   79

Express Lane   —   82

Aftermath   —   84

Plenty   —   86

Acknowledgments   —   *89*

IN EVERY SEAM

Summers on Screvin

Big Wheels would crunch their noise
as preschoolers rode those oversized tricycles
past every house on the block, continuously
underfoot. No one wanted training wheels

on a brand-new, just-out-of-the-box
three-speed bike, but everyone wanted
neon yo-yos that glowed in the dark,
wanted those pink balls the color

of bubble gum, perfect for a sweaty game
of handball against the back of someone's
house. When bored with freeze tag,
with red light, green light, 1-2-3,

we'd blow giant bubbles through
huge plastic hoops, draw hopscotch
on the ground in colored chalk,
or crouch low to play jacks,

coveting those silver sparks.
Certain possessions weren't easy
to share: rusty metal skates
that fit over sneakers just

right, Hula Hoops and skateboards
no one else had played with yet,
wooden paddles with cherry red
rubber balls attached by strings.

We could spend all day bouncing
those balls off their paddles,
counting every time each ball
leapt off, sprung back.

We lived for water: water balloons,
water pistols, lawn sprinklers,
and hoses. Open fire hydrants
poured rivers into the streets

and we danced in rushing water
until someone turned it off,
told us to do something better
with ourselves, so we stirred

up mud at curbs, digging
rich silt with Popsicle sticks,
grabbed handfuls of dandelions,
fingers coated with that sticky

green juice, or scaled rocks
in the open lot across the street,
jumped on a rank soggy mattress
as if it were a trampoline,

and not some sorry piece of garbage
someone had dumped among bushes,
ran home with scraped knees
and dirty bruised legs

when we heard the piddly music
of the ice-cream truck, craving
the sweet shaved ice of sno-cones.
Tired, we'd sit on the hood

of someone's idle car
until they yelled at us
to get off, adults scolding
from their lawn chairs

as they traded cigarettes and gossip,
cooking summer barbecue outdoors,
sharp smoke rising thick and hot
from coal-darkened grills.

They'd offer us cold sodas
and salty potato chips,
chicken legs with the thighs
still on, sauce dripping

onto paper plates and napkins,
our mouths and fingers greasy;
happy, clothes so dirty and torn
our mothers would soon make rags

of them, muscles sore as we
gulped, chewed, and swallowed
all the food anyone gave us, sure
we could never eat enough, never be satisfied.

On Sidewalks, on Street Corners, as Girls

Just who was Miss Mary Mack,
all dressed in black, with her stalwart buttons
up and down her back, her patient request
for fifty cents to see some bedraggled circus elephant
jump a fence? As children, we never asked
who she was, content instead to clap out her story
in pairs, our hands meeting, then parting
in quick motions. When we sang
We're going to Kentucky, we're going to the fair,
to see the señorita with flowers in her hair,
we'd shake our little girl hips in time
with the melody, but we never stopped to ask
what a lovely *señorita* was doing at a fair,
and we possessed no knowledge of where
Kentucky was, didn't even know
what one did at a fair—children who only
knew cinder block and cement,
corner storefronts, brick high rises.
We sang about Miss Lucy
and her prized steamboat,
the steamboat destined for heaven
and Miss Lucy for hell;
sang *rumble to the bottom,*
rumble to the top,
one girl in the midst of the circle
twirling and twirling until she stopped,
finger pointed at the next girl
who would shake her stuff in front
of us, our chants heard in every

school yard, every parking lot,
everywhere small dark girls
could gather to hear their voices swell
in nonsense rhyme, neighborhood chant.
Hands and feet would stomp out rhythms
inherited from older sisters—story-songs
about seeing London, seeing France,
sassy songs about someone's mama
doing wrong, acting crazy.
No one would dare take away
our homemade street-corner music,
so we'd spend every afternoon after school
and every shred of summer daylight
riffing, scatting, improvising,
unafraid to tell each other
shake it to the east,
shake it to the west,
shake it to the one
you love the best.

Traitor

What did that girl on the playground mean
when she hissed *you ain't black* at me,

pigtails bouncing, her hands
on her bony hips? She sucked her teeth,

stared at me with such contempt
that I wanted to hide in my mother's

skirts, wanted to scurry to my house's
hall closet, safe among the great

dark coats. *You talk funny,* she said,
all proper, as if pronunciation

was a sin, a scandal, a strike
against the race only a traitor

would perform, an Uncle Tom sellout.
Somehow I'd let her down by not

slurring, I'd failed her by not
letting language laze on its own,

its sound unhurried. I'd said
isn't rather than *ain't,*

called my mother *mom* instead
of *momma,* pronounced *th* distinctly

so no one would confuse *them*
with *dem, those* with *dose.*

Your momma talk that funny?
the girl demanded, her face

in my face now, her nose
inches from mine, her eyes

lit by something near hate,
but more ferocious, a kind

of disgust mixed with pity,
disdain. *We're from Canada,*

I said, and the girl's eyes
went wide, as if I'd said

cantaloupe, or *harpoon,*
or some nonsense word like

*abracadabra. There must not be
no black folks in Canada then,*

she sneered, leaning in further,
pushing on my chest with one

bony finger, pinning me there
like a bug to a fly screen,

pressing me so hard that
my lower lip started to tremble

on its own, a sign of weakness
she laughed a mocking, heavy

laugh at, telling me *go on and cry,
white girl, cry till your momma*

can hear, pushing me so I toppled
onto my back, ripping the pants

my mother warned me not to rip.
She stood over me, laughing

like she'd just seen the world's
best clown, laughing though I

was just as dark as she,
my hair in the same

nappy plaits, my skin
the same rough brown.

Urban Games

When the game was polite
we called it run, catch, and kiss—
boys and girls pursuing each other
down and up bumpy sidewalks,
trying to plaster kisses
on any visible body part:
a leg, knee, but preferably
on the forehead or cheek,
those expanses of brown skin
that grew shiny-slick
as we ran the summer streets.
But I preferred the more
violent variation—run, catch,
and *kill,* that game's object
direct, brutal—simply run
as fast as possible with fists
ready to pummel, hoping
to catch whichever boy
had teased you mercilessly
that week—mocking your
high-water pants, ugly
no-brand sneakers your mama
bought for a dollar ninety-nine
at Woolworth's. That chase
would pull the breath from
your body, lungs issuing fire,
burning as you ran, as you
reached out your arms to grab
a sleeve, an ankle, a wrist.

And when you finally caught someone
you could punch his arms hard,
double him up on the cement
until he couldn't take anymore,
though some boys would claim
no girl's punches could ever
keep them down, yelling it
as they wriggled away, elusive.
God forbid a boy should
catch you, happy to hit
your arms until welts appeared,
rising on shoulders, shins.
In summertime playgrounds
and parks, away from adults
and school, this cruelty
sustained us all day long,
this game far more intricate
than freeze tag, hopscotch.
Raggedy boys and girls,
we loved to see each other
suffer, unable to leave someone
on the sidewalk to nurse
sore arms, bruised thighs,
unable to resist one last punch.

Malice

That Stephanie thought
she was the cutest girl
on the fifth-grade playground

with her big brown eyes
and button-cute nose,
hair pressed and curled

into bouncy ringlets tied
by long streaks of ribbon,
her prematurely developed body

squeezed into tight pants and tops
that all the boys loved,
and all the girls despised.

Rumor had it she'd strip
for any boy who asked,
her tight jeans on the bathroom floor

whenever they wished, brown body
up against theirs, panties tossed aside.
We girls without curves or curls

loved to talk evil about her,
spreading gossip that she liked
to touch boys without their pants on,

that she'd make them line up
one by one after school, make them
unzip their flies so she could

do whatever she wanted for as long
as she wanted, her lips not tiring,
hands skilled. Her body gave her away,

we claimed, jealous when we saw her
walk the halls at school, her womanish hips
swaying, rear end moving to a rhythm

beyond our understanding.
Even our male teacher noticed,
picking her first to run errands,

deliver messages, his eyes
steady on her thighs as she walked
from the room. So did we cry

when she did, did we run
to comfort her that day
she wore a dress to school

and six boys cornered her
back where the chain-link fence
kept the school yard from the alleyway?

Did any girl tell Stephanie *sorry*
after we heard her sobs and shouts,
saw her trying to fight them off,

her eyes teary and sore,
curls coming loose each time
another boy tried to reach

beneath her dress to pull
her underwear down? We had
no explanations or apologies

when our teacher demanded to know
why no one helped her, not caring
if he raged at us, appalled.

He could tell our parents,
we didn't care—we were too busy
savoring how homely Stephanie looked—

cute face swollen, cheeks puffy,
tear stained, eyes as red
as the perky little dress

she'd worn to school that day—
buttons in a neat row down its front,
its pleats just as sharp as could be.

Five and Dime

Otherwise known as McCrory's,
the neighborhood discount variety store
filled with junky merchandise
that looked even shabbier
under the circling dust motes
and buzzing fluorescent lights.

The store manager would stomp
down the humid crowded aisles,
his pock marked face unhappy,
lower lip twisted in spite,
his hefty, lurching gait
showing no respect for that store,

that neighborhood where Spanish
floated in and out of doorways all day
and night, where the pizza shops sold
spicy beef patties, fizzy Jamaican ginger beer.
He'd snarl at all the tan and brown bodies
that came in and out of his glass doors every day,

those people always asking their questions,
touching every item for sale, leaving
fingerprints on the makeup, the school supplies,
stains on the ill-fitting clothes.
One of those children
he hated most, I'd linger for hours

among the jars of hair grease
and straightening combs,
among lipsticks too bright
or too brown, too purple
or too red. I'd pick things up,
put them down, grab combs

or plastic barrettes, ponytail holders
or bobby pins, decide I didn't want
any of them, then open giant bottles
of watery shampoo or bubble bath,
sniffing to tell if they really
smelled of strawberries or bubble gum.

Maybe he thought I'd steal
a pencil sharpener or a package
of ball-points, that I'd slip
a pair of phony silver earrings
into my schoolbag, slide a slender
perfume bottle into my pocket. But I

didn't care what he thought,
I touched whatever I wanted to touch,
ran sticky fingers over wrinkled
corduroy pants and no-name jeans,
chintzy cotton T-shirts
and neon jogging suits.

Knowing I wasn't going to buy
anything more than a thirty-cent pack
of gum, he suspected my pockets
were crammed with stolen goods,
so he came at me, grabbed my shoulder
with one broad, stubby hand,

bumpy face down close as he demanded
to know where my mother was, shaking me,
checking my pockets, my bag. *Don't you dare
come back in here without your mother,* he spat,
pushing me out onto the sidewalk in front
of that friendly discount store, that place for values.

Playing Rough

Oh what a vicious game
they encouraged us to play:
two teams of scraggly school kids
lined up at opposite ends

of the gym to face each other,
each kid on line taking turns
firing a red rubber ball
to see whom they could hit,

how hard—could you make someone
cry, hit them on the side
of the face, on the nose,
in the eye? Our bodies

were barely covered by thin
uniforms—faded yellow T-shirts,
skimpy blue shorts, sneakers,
knees and thighs exposed,

upper arms and elbows sure spots
for blows from a speeding ball.
What was the point of this game
other than learning how to move

before the ball struck you,
than learning how to launch a ball
with all your hate mustered behind
the movement? Maybe our teachers

thought us too young and dumb
for anything more complex,
too stupid for basketball,
volleyball, maybe they were

too lazy to teach us anything
besides this cruel game of catch,
this mean-spirited competition—
sometimes boys against girls,

sometimes bigger kids against
smaller. But usually there wasn't
any sense to it; all they had to do
was make sure we left the line

if we were hit, one point for the other
team. Everyone jeered if a kid
couldn't dodge the ball, if he
wasn't quick enough to scurry

out of the way, if she wasn't
paying attention and the ball
thudded her right between
the shoulders, knocking her

breathless. So that kid
would sit in the bleachers
after being struck from
the game: head down, shoulders

low, promising to be crueler
next time, to fire the ball
harder, send more people down
before being knocked out.

The team with one person left
was somehow the winner,
that particular boy or girl
exhilarated, the rest of us

too glum by then to care
who'd won, sulky as we lined up
to go back to the locker rooms
where at least we could be evil

on our terms, use our fists
instead of that silly ball,
deciding for ourselves
whom to hit and why,

instead of waiting
for some crude gym teacher
to shout at us to begin,
puffing his whistle shrill.

Arts and Crafts

Juicy Magic Markers leaking their ink,
staining hands red, green, and blue
for days, tempera paint poured thick

from jars for fingertips to play in,
to make wet, sticky portraits of glowing trees
and flying houses, gold and silver glitter

I would pour on anything, including
my shirt, my shorts, my shoes.
This is what I want to remember

from every day camp, youth group
or after-school program I was ever
sent to, from every school period devoted

to the single-minded pursuit
of arts and crafts, a discipline
that combined one clean room,

one severely underpaid teacher,
several boxes of art supplies,
and thirty-three antsy, eager kids.

Nothing was ever understated—
not the bold waxy crayons
that were thick as two fingers,

not the easels with their generous
clean swaths of paper, not the brushes
with their stiff brittle bristles.

Our aim was to make something pretty
from something useful, to turn tissue paper
and pipe cleaners into bouquets of pink

roses, transform paper plates into
ritual masks, chewing gum wrappers
into high-fashion jewelry, change

worn-out socks into hand puppets,
buttons sewed on for eyes. Only
our determination could make

dull safety scissors cut through
construction paper, only our persistence
could make sweaty gray lumps of clay

into glazed and burnished ashtrays.
Watercolors, colored pencils, paste,
beads, ribbon, and yarn all made

the world slow down, go away,
each project more intense
than the one before, more elaborate,

one requiring shells, shellac, and macaroni
all at once, everyone taking home
some bit of handmade beauty—some

animal sewn from shiny fabric,
one limb shorter than its others,
some kite fashioned from a paper bag

and Popsicle sticks, some rag doll formed
from an ugly dress no one wore, the garment
redeemed by paint, string, rubber bands.

Barbie's Little Sister

How terrible it would be
to be Barbie's little sister,
suspended in perpetual pre-adolescence
while Barbie, hair flying behind her
in a tousled blonde mane, dashed
from adventure to adventure,
ready for space travel or calf roping
or roller disco in campy, flashy clothes
that defied good taste and reason.
Stuck with the awful nickname Skipper,
Barbie's little sis never got out much,
a mere boarder in Barbie's three-story
hot-pink Dream House, too young
to wear the thousands of outfits
stashed in the bedroom closets:
purple beaded Armani evening gowns,
knit sweater dresses by Donna Karan,
specially commissioned tennis togs
sewn personally by Oleg Cassini.
Skipper had to buy off the rack
at K-Mart, condemned to wear
floral sunsuits with Peter Pan collars.
Unlike her bosomy sister,
Skipper had no chest
for the boys to ogle,
until some bright toy maker
gave us Growing Up Skipper:
with a twist of her right arm,
she grew taller, breasts sprouting
where there once were none,

a thick rubber band inside her
pushing her chest up and out
until the band snapped
and Skipper was stuck at age fifteen,
never the same again.
For consolation, she turned to
Barbie's black friend Christie—
who was just figuring out
all the fuss about equal rights—
and Barbie's best pal Midge,
who was tired of hearing
about spats with Ken, knowing
he was cheating on America's sweetheart
with every new celebrity doll on the market—
Brooke Shields, Cher, Dorothy Hamill.
Together, those three decided
they'd had enough of Toyland—
so they pooled their cash,
swiped Barbie's camper,
and tore out of California
for Las Vegas, where they bought
a little establishment not too far
from the gaming houses,
a restaurant for all of us
without thick manes of hair
or upturned noses, without
impossibly slender ankles
and tiny feet, without
perfectly molded breasts.

Funny Pages

Did anyone actually ever like
Archie comics, the town of Riverdale
filled with teenagers too dense
to ever graduate, eternally worried

about the malt shop's cheeseburgers,
about days at old Riverdale High
with that balding, bumbling principal,
that sappy spinster teacher,

pointer clutched in her skinny hand?
What zone did these cheery freaks
occupy, too wholesome and decent
to be believed—Betty with her

bouncy blonde ponytail and boundless
hope that one day Archie would wise up,
go out with only her; Veronica,
with her huffy rich-bitch mean streak,

penchant for spending her daddy's
long green at every opportunity;
Jughead, with his dopey slouch
and endless appetite? What

unmet childhood need was he trying
to satisfy with all that meat,
that many buns? Did anyone
think they were funny?

Did anyone think Archie
was funny—his hayseed red hair
and hokey letter sweaters,
his goofy ignorance of women?

Betty swooned her good-girl swoon,
but he didn't notice; Veronica
paid him no heed until he showed
up on her rival's arm, Betty's perky

charm winning him over for just
one date. The only character
worth anything was Reggie,
evil, spoiled, antisocial Reggie,

with his fast, sleek car
and sullen attitude, his vivid
contempt for Archie's constant grin,
hatred for that broken-down

jalopy Archie tooled around in
as if it were special, divine.
In the real world, every kid
in school would want to be

Reggie's friend, not Archie's,
everyone would want a ride
in that shiny sports car,
everyone would want a chance

to get Reggie's money out
from under him, cajoling him
with compliments, trying
to get him to share his wealth,

and no one would want to hang out
at that damn soda fountain,
waiting for Veronica and Betty
to come in the door. In the

real world, we'd grab Reggie's
wallet, swipe the keys to his coupe,
and tear the hell out of Riverdale,
driving as fast and as far as possible

from football games and homecomings,
hot dogs and hamburgers, root beer floats
and Friday night school dances, from
eerie cheerleaders who never grow old.

Fishing

My bamboo pole was really plastic
coated to look like wood, its paint
a gold-brown shellac that hardly
fooled anyone. Though he'd never

read the book, Dad called it
my Huck Finn pole, teasing me
about all I'd catch with it,
laughing and bragging as we

stood on the dock at Rye Beach,
casting our lines into rough,
gray waters that moved so sluggishly
beneath us. I tried to have patience

for this fishing, the ocean's chill
making me shiver deep, tried to love
the waiting the same way my father
did, but hated it all—loathed

my flimsy pole, tired of hoping
for a tug on its cheap plastic bobber,
recoiled from the wriggling, smelly bait
Dad had bought a full bucket of,

the fat worms coiling, uncoiling.
I wanted to flee to Rye Playland
instead, sneak onto the roller coaster
while no one was watching, buy

huge mounds of dense pink cotton candy
with the quarters that jingled
in my pockets. I wanted anything else
but to stand all day on a shaky dock,

watching Dad's mood darken when no fish
took his bait, wanted that so much
that I almost didn't notice
when my pole started to shake,

some sad and stupid fish
nibbling my tattered worm.
Pull 'em in, Dad yelled,
but the damn pole was too limp,

not strong enough for any fish
bigger than a finger. When Dad
felt a tug on his line,
I saw him bite his lip,

straining to land this one,
pulling his arms back and back
until the fish landed on the dock,
its slick scales mottled gray

and brown, gills rasping.
Triumphant, Dad whacked its head
with a tightly rolled *Daily News,*
telling me to pull the hook

when it finally stopped flopping.
Sickened, fascinated, I shuddered
to touch that coarse fish
mouth, working and ripping

the tiny wire loose, seeing
how the struggle bent it
out of shape, but left it
intact, snagged in that slimy jaw.

Bribery

We had a job to do, April and I,
had to stop at every apartment
of practically every building

in the projects, stooping to stuff fliers
beneath each bullet-resistant steel door,
dashing away before snarling tenants

could unlock all their locks, stick
their heads out into the dim hallways
to yell at us damn kids who'd dare

slide this garbage into their homes.
My father had promised us five bucks apiece
if we would spend our Saturday

distributing his flyers to each floor
in those twenty-story tenements,
so we took the elevators all the way up,

raced down each set of cinderblock stairs,
stopping to do as we'd been told, sliding flyers
for Everest Advertising into homes of people

who probably had no desire to do business,
no need for pens or pencils or calendars
on which my father's firm would print any message,

any slogan, any logo. Who had the money
in these coarse-walled concrete buildings
to pay for such dubious expertise;

did my father honestly think someone would call
wanting to order two dozen T-shirts,
a half-dozen boxes of buttons?

I don't know now, didn't care then,
and neither did April, both of us
thinking that five dollars could

snag us everything we wanted—
all the candy and chips we could
munch, all the sweet crumbly

cookies, moist cupcakes. And we
thought my father was such a big man
with his own business, his own fliers,

his five-dollar bills he'd
only give us after hours of work—
our legs aching, hearts thudding from

too many close calls with growling German
shepherds. He held our bills above our heads,
teasing, trying to make us grab at them,

but we were too tired, our greed spent
as we walked April back to her building,
my father exclaiming about all the new clients

this trick would bring in, scheming his next
stunt, the next piece of his master plan
that would make him rich, a man

no longer reliant on two twelve-
year-old girls, a sales force
who could only work weekends.

Artist-in-Residence

Good ghetto girls and boys
get art if they're lucky:
field trips downtown for kids
whose parents cared little
about the finer things —
sculptures, paintings, ballets,
Shakespearean plays to enrich
our inner-city minds,
to fascinate and calm us
in ways the streets could not.
So not one of us was surprised
when a lanky white woman named Sylvia
showed up at school to teach us dance,
her long brown hair parted straight
down the middle, then braided
so it hung heavily down her back,
leaping if she leapt, turned.
She dressed in weird, loose clothes
tie-dyed in colors I later
learned the names of —
lavender, chartreuse, azure —
wore dainty Chinese slippers
that slid and slipped easily
over industrial-strength school tile.
She charmed us, this white woman,
with her wide and slightly bucktoothed smile,
her long arms that flailed above her head
as she implored us to reach, grow steady
as trees, our shoes off, piled

in a corner, chairs and tables pushed aside
for this once-a-week dance session
that wasn't really dance,
but more like awkward mime,
our bodies mimicking hers
as she spun, crouched,
transforming herself to hissing
witch, generous fairy.
She made us reenact
the myth of Pandora's box,
so one lucky girl got to be Pandora
while the rest of us were down
on all fours, ready to spring
from our invisible box, ready
to dance all the evil in the world.
When that chosen girl leaned over,
peered in, and opened up that box,
we all flew out hooting, screaming,
rushing at her while Sylvia clapped
to the prerecorded drumming coming
from her portable tape recorder.
She smiled to see us whirl
as if she'd really done something,
taught us something about how
evil moves, temptation works.
We never told her how embarrassing
we all thought it was, never
let her know how strange we thought
her dances were, how lily white

and out of style. We let her think
she hadn't wasted her time with us,
clinging to her when her half hour
was up, chanting her name aloud
when class was over, thirty-five
underprivileged voices singing
Sylvia, Sylvia, Sylvia!

It's Tough to Be a Girl Scout in the City

especially when practically every girl in the troop
goes to Holy Family Catholic School, and you go
to Henry Hudson Junior High, so practically every
girl in the troop thinks she's better than you,
her parents willing to pay for her education.

You've let Yvette talk you into yet another initiation,
this one seemingly less perilous than the baton twirling club
she took you to—dozens of girls catching and twirling batons
in an apartment building's rec room, some persistent
despite being bonked in the head by batons speeding

their way down. You're hoping this joining will be different,
that you'll make friends besides Yvette, who seems to have
no trouble talking their talk, knowing their slang.
With no prior history of scouting, you join at the
Cadette level, a dangerous time when hormones and cattiness

are just kicking in, pimples erupting across your nose
just in time for Saturday's troop meeting, where you
work toward sewing badges by piecing together fabric
cut into bunny shapes, then stuffing the results.
You like this work: the large embroidery needle,

the yarn you use as thread, the precut patterns that are
virtually foolproof, so that everyone takes home individual
variations on the same calico rabbit. In weeks to come,
you earn badges in Personal Hygiene, in Reading,
in Needlework. And because there is no camp nearby,

the troop settles on a trip to Flushing Meadow Park,
running relay races in the untamed splendor of Queens,
your Physical Fitness badge only a third-place finish away,
the day full of sprints, dashes, a race where two girls
stumble toward the finish line tied together at the ankles.

Even this you don't mind, careful to sew that badge on first
on an old green vest you now use as your uniform's vest,
though you wish the uniforms were any other color than green.
But slowly, over the following weeks, the troop's one concern
becomes a dance routine the girls from Holy Family

already know—intricate steps they perform in formation
so that one misstep is all the more noticeable. You're
the only girl in the troop who consistently messes up,
so you end up apologizing when you turn at the wrong time—
facing left when everyone else on line is facing right,

turning right when everyone else has turned left.
As far as you can tell, this dancing serves no purpose
other than humiliation, fulfilling the requirements
for no badge listed in your handbook. But you practice
with them, vainly, hope they'll stop soon, until

one Saturday they decide they'll perform this routine
for their parents, in sky-blue leotards everyone
must wear. But that Saturday you forget your leotard,
forget the steps, so that the girls from Holy Family
think you're a loser who can't follow directions

or dance, and you wonder why these girls can't follow
the handbook's simple credo: *Be a sister to your fellow
Girl Scout.* They'd rather laugh instead
at your public school clumsiness, your slow,
uncoordinated feet. So you toss your green vest

far in back of your closet, spend Saturday
mornings at home in front of the TV,
earning hours toward a badge you're sure
they don't have—the badge of nonattendance,
of teen sloth and laziness that has you

sprawled out on the floor, staring up
at twenty-five-year-old cartoons on the old
black-and-white, stuffing salty popcorn
into your mouth in handfuls, refusing anyone's calls,
especially Yvette's, the room yours alone, without sisters.

My Father's Heroes

Not JFK, not MLK,
certainly not Ronald Reagan
or Edward I. Koch,
no, instead my father
chose to glory in the feats
of Cool Papa Bell, quickest
man in the Negro Leagues,
able, Dad bragged,
to flick off a light switch,
then dart into bed
before the room went dark.
Praising the fast-dancing feet
of the Nicholas brothers,
he called my attention to
their rapid-fire acrobatics,
but saved his true love
for Peg Leg Bates,
the one-legged tap dancer
who'd pound out a furious rhythm
on his wooden leg,
dazzling audiences
with leaps, hops, bounds.
I never saw Father
anywhere near a piano,
but he still schooled me
about Jimmy Rushing—
"Mister Five by Five,"
tagged so because
he stood five feet tall
and looked five feet wide,

had me humming Jelly Roll Morton's
creole jazz though he'd never
been near New Orleans,
made certain I knew the difference
between Fats Domino and Fats Waller,
played me the Harlem rhapsodies
of Ellington so loudly I thought
the orchestra had come to visit,
Sir Duke himself in our living
room, elegant in top hat, tails.
To Dad, Satchmo and Satchel Paige
both deserved equal praise;
equal adulation was given
to the theatrics of Louie Jordan
as he belted out rhythm-and-blues tunes
about hard-headed women like "Caldonia,"
the hi-de-ho of Cab Calloway
as he spun tales of "Minnie the Moocher,"
regal in yards of zoot suit,
and to the sublime grace of Mr. B,
Billy Eckstine crooning smoother
than any white man.
Coleman Hawkins, Lester Young,
Bird and Diz all came to play
from our raspy console hi-fi,
its needle worn, jumping over scratches.

But some mornings,
I'd wake to hear a woman's voice
filling our rooms with trembling

love songs, a voice so vulnerable
even I understood, even though
the language was French,
the singer white, female.
This, he'd say, *is Piaf,*
the little sparrow,
and I'd listen to that voice
send its sorrows through our house
and I knew that what touched my father
wasn't always race, wasn't always color.
Somehow he knew I needed
to hear this woman sing
from her fragile bones,
her sound silencing us both,
as her crowds in Paris must have been
when they saw her tiny figure
on the stage, bent over to sing
the last vestiges of a ballad,
the last words
she'd give them.

The Tenant

Teddy Reed, our luckless tenant,
lived downstairs in a marijuana haze,
that sweet sharp scent rising up and out
of the one-bedroom apartment he rented
from my tightfisted father.
Months before, his wife and child
had left him behind, though mail
still came for Pamela Reed,
the Reed family, Mr. and Mrs. Reed.
What did he do down there all day
besides inhaling that acrid smoke,
the apartment now stripped of
the baby's things, his wife's
dresses and blouses no longer
dangling in the closet? He wasn't
circling want ads—the first
of every month he'd sheepishly
trudge upstairs, ask to speak
to my father. I'd look at him,
wondering how anyone's eyes
could stay that glassy and slick,
that red, corneas crisscrossed
by spidery lines. My father
would rage at him so loudly
that I thought—no, I swore—
the house would erupt,
his anger more potent than usual
when Reed would come to tell him
of another thirty days' worth

of bad luck: his brother was supposed
to send money, but didn't,
a mysterious check never arrived,
the job he had been sure of
went to another man. My father
might have strangled him
had he not been so sad-sack thin,
pitiful, but he swung a cutlass
in front of Reed instead,
warning, *See this? It chopped
cane in the islands, imagine
what it could do to you.*
He'd push Teddy Reed back downstairs
for another month, until one month
he finally had enough, gave him
two weeks to pack, be gone.

But Reed wasn't as fragile
as he looked, not as numb
as I thought, because before he left
that dim-lit one-bedroom apartment,
he turned on every faucet,
making sure the wooden floors
would become fully waterlogged
so they'd warp and bend until
no amount of sanding could
make them smooth again.
Teddy Reed took his few things—
his stereo, his army fatigues, his stash—
and went who knows where,

laughing hearty and loud
whenever he thought of what
my father saw when he opened
that door, saw the damage done
to the walls, sinks, floors,
knowing my father's anger
could never touch him again.

Day-Tripping

In that dark classroom,
we watched frame after frame
of antidrug filmstrips,
cartoons some genius invented
to scare us straight,
keep us from mind-blowing
temptations, each gaudy scene
chronicling the adventures
of some poor animated sap
who couldn't resist the stranger
who sidled up to him
on the playground, offering
handfuls of tiny glossy
blue and red pills. Stupid fool,
he thought they were candy,
swallowed them easily,
tossing uppers into his mouth,
his big cartoon character head
swelling as he took off
on his two wheeler,
trying to fly, pumping the pedals
faster and faster, only to careen
into a white garden gate,
a scenario someone somewhere
thought would scare us.
But the blond fool on his toy bike
only set us to laughing,
giggles erupting all around
the room, our teacher

demanding quiet, refusing
to move that fine little film
forward until we shut up.
By the time we hushed,
Blondie was back at the
playground, his friend
from the day before back again
dressed in the same platform shoes,
wide lapels, bell-bottoms.
Something to calm you down,
he whispered, leaning in
to put eight nine ten pills
in the little idiot's hands.
He stuffed them all down,
walked home to mother and dad
only to fall asleep
over family dinner,
dreaming into his mashed potatoes.
Mother was shocked, but knew
it was drugs, and when her boy
came to, they hugged,
their big cartoony mouths
open wide to warn us
about strange men who offer
pretty candies to boys and girls.
Turning the film off,
the lights back on,
our teacher asked *any questions
now that you've stopped laughing,*

her face severe, unsmiling,
arms crossed rigid
over her bony chest,
and Kevin, sprawled in the back row,
sneakers up on my desk,
slurred, *Where can I find me a man*
who won't make me pay nothin'
for all the shit I want?

Motives

Just why my father rescued
that limping ragged kitten
I'll never know—he didn't
like pets, banned them
from our house, claimed

they'd only claw and tear
our sofas and chairs,
ruin our carpets. But
he managed to coax
that scared scrawny cat

from beneath our car,
cooing her into daylight,
into a shoe box lined
with day-old papers.
I pretended no interest,

busied myself with TV
instead, Prince Charles
and Lady Diana pledging
perfect marital love
before the whole world,

wedding finery not hiding
that she was plain, he
was ugly, no beauty
in their royalty. But I did
peek outside, saw my father

holding that box close,
murmuring to calm
the squirming, shivering
cat, his voice low, steady,
not the bark that made me jump

when he came home from work
impatient, ill tempered.
He turned her loose
in the living room,
let her feel her way

along the carpet, let her creep
between the sofa and the wall,
her bruised leg trailing
behind, damp wet spots
pooling in her wake.

A spasm stiffened her,
killed her, gray fur matted.
So much for trying to save
anything, the shoe box filled
then flung into the trash,

stains on the rugs
not coming out, though
I scrubbed. So much for princes
and princesses, for their palace
guards, horse-drawn carriages.

So much for my father,
who didn't make me love him
any more or any less
by stroking her one minute,
laughing at her death

the next, his motives his own,
his rages and silences and outbursts
witnessed by a daughter who had no love
for princes or princesses,
no use for cats.

The Swimming Pool

I know I never actually swam there,
the water so murky green my mother
forbade me from going in it, not even

allowing me to wade in the shallow end
where dusky water lapped cracked
and mossy tiles. But I didn't mind,

was there for the scenery—the tall,
brown, seventeen-year-old lifeguards
who patrolled the slippery edges

of the pool, their chests smooth, as if
polished, legs lightly muscled, then tapering
down to slender, powerful ankles

that I wanted to touch even then,
even though I was thirteen, flat-chested,
so skinny I feared my ribs would poke through

my suit. Even then I wanted to spend hours
admiring those backs and thighs, giggled
behind my hands whenever my girlfriends

said that word, describing what lay beneath
those taut swim trunks Ricky, Sean,
and Lionel wore as they broke up fights

between snot-nosed younger boys,
returned weepy lost children to their mothers.
We girls would lie by the pool on towels

stolen from home, pretending the lifeguards
where there for our pleasure only, speculating
on whether or not they had girlfriends,

showing each other what lifeguard kisses
were like, demonstrating on the backs
of our hands, lips pressed on that skin.

What happened after those deep kisses
we weren't exactly sure, but knew
it all had something to do

with that word that made us laugh so long
and so hard. We didn't have the nerve
to truly talk to them, too afraid

to say anything but hi, too unworldly
to know what else to say to boys
older than the gawky monsters

in our classes, those fools
who snapped our bras, then ran
down school corridors yelling

training bra, training bra!
Desperate, we thought it might work,
so we headed for the public bathrooms,

took rolls from each stall
and stuffed scratchy wads of toilet paper
down the front of each suit, hoping

that would age us, make us wise
and beautiful as prom queens.
And we each picked a lifeguard

to go talk to, to charm with our
newfound wealth. I picked Ricky,
with his long-lashed eyes

and tiny waist, his chiseled stomach.
But as I walked to him I slipped,
fell right in that dangerous water,

its raucous chlorine stinging,
filling my nose, burning my throat.
Ricky pulled me out, kind enough

not to say anything about the soggy paper
that clung to my chest like seaweed,
silent as I sputtered, choking,

heaving to get that nasty water out.
I didn't know where my friends were,
didn't care, didn't want to ever return

to that pool again, teeth chattering
as I coughed and shivered, shaking
water from my ears, flinging

wads of paper from my chest,
not caring where they landed,
not caring if anyone saw me.

Señora Williams

would have liked to rap our knuckles
whenever we conveniently left
our homework home, the strenuous *tarea*
she assigned as if we had no other class
but fifth-period Intermediate Spanish

with a *profesora* who ranted ceaselessly
when we didn't roll our *r*'s, when we
insisted on making silent *h* audible.
Scowling, she walked the narrow rows
between desks, demanding to see our

verb conjugations, our primitive answers
to the textbook's facile questions,
snapping if we left one off,
blank spaces so repellent to her
she'd stand by our desks to punish

us, firing off vocabulary drills,
mocking us when we couldn't remember
the most basic verbs: *ser,* to be,
volver, to return, *ver,* to see,
rompier, to break. She wanted

to break us, so she prodded,
badgered, jumped up and down,
her massive curly bouffant
immobile, powder and rouge
heavy on her puffy face,

her frown bright in ruby lipstick.
She'd single people out, make them
stand to read aloud, charging forward
if they refused, ready for
una lucha grande every time.

Once she singled out Teresa
one too many times, trying
to make her learn, forcing
her answers, asking, *¿como se dice
"dress"? ¿como se dice "shirt"?*

¿como se dice "pants"? whacking her ruler
on Teresa's desk with each question,
glaring as Teresa refused to reply.
Señora Williams banged
that ruler three more times,

harder each time until Teresa
grabbed it, broke it, yelled
¿como se dice "bitch"?,
her accent perfect in anger.
Señora Williams screamed *get out,*

and Teresa slammed her books,
mouthed *fuck you* as she left,
the class cheering her on
silently, knowing there'd be
pages and pages of homework

because of this, *mas verbos,*
mas preguntas, more hours hating
that woman who called us all
perezoso, so lazy she couldn't teach us
anything, not even if she died trying.

Life Science

What did we ever learn
in those humid, musty classrooms,
each lab reeking of too much
formaldehyde, too many solvents,

sinks and counter tops
coated in gritty, dusty film
from too many scrubbings,
too much scouring powder?

We learned patience, yes,
fingers timid on slides
that just might break
from a single slight tap,

on test tubes that might shatter
if not held just the right way,
passed carefully from partner
to partner, on petri dishes

that had to stay sealed
against the taint of air,
prized bacteria growing thick
on gummy-smooth agar.

We learned through trial,
but mostly error—flames
on Bunsen burners leaping
way too high, only to sputter

out, beakers set too close
to the edges of the tables,
only to be knocked to the floor,
plastic safety goggles strapped

too tightly around some hapless
student's head, pressing hard
on that poor skull. Whether
we wanted to or not, we learned

poise—coping with microscopes
whose knobs wouldn't turn,
with fetal pigs gone hard,
rubbery, organs no longer

distinct, immobile frogs stuck
to dissecting trays, faded
to tattered bits, plucked
by too many tweezers.

No one to blame but ourselves
when an experiment went awry:
too much stain on the specimen,
not enough light through

the microscope, too many cells
huddled on one slide,
paramecium too abundant,
swimming their one-celled lives

straight out of our field of vision.
But when we managed to stain
a slide just right, not too much violet
on the darting protozoa,

we whooped like silly children,
jubilant to see the details
our thick texts illustrated
so lavishly: membranes

and vacuoles, shaky cytoplasm
quivering even under low power.
We diagramed what we saw,
confident in our methods,

our data not rigged for once,
but charted in multiple inks,
documented in neat columns,
tabulated in strict pages.

The Art of Vallejo

> Here is the stuff of myths and visions, the kinds of primal image that exert a powerful pull on all of us. The subjects of Boris Vallejo's paintings do not exist in the real world. There are no living models for the characters and creatures or the exotic backgrounds his art depicts.
> —from *The Fantastic Art of Boris Vallejo*

These bodies are the bodies
every heavy-breathing teenage boy
supposedly desires:
long-legged space vixens
so curvaceous and firm
they haunt the eye, supplanting
what real women look like
with visions of brawny temptresses
on winged steeds, sailing past
blazing planets with swords
drawn, hair fanning out.
Vallejo's women fight
rough-tusked elephants,
tame giant lions, perch
on prehistoric lizards,
clad in freaky chain-link gold bikinis,
high-heeled black leather boots,
bow and arrow in one hand,
spiked ball on a chain
gripped in the other.
I don't know who would challenge
these sci-fi women warriors,

these physical cartoons of
female form: their chests thrust
forward, breasts brazen, nearly naked,
their calves tight, teeming
with taut, heavy muscles,
arms wrapped in bracelets
from wrists to forearm.
His women grace covers
of comic books and paperbacks,
fantasies pitched under boys' beds,
pulp novels with titles to match:
Primeval Princess, Nubian Warrior, The Amazon's Pet.

Any good feminist
would call these images porn,
products of a fevered male mind
full of slave girls and snarling cats.
But Vallejo's women wield chains, whips,
sharp daggers with long blades,
chasing ferocious beasts, risking
the wrath of savage aliens.
Suspended between galaxies,
they coast from world to world
on star-roving ships,
medieval chariots.
And the best of them look
like they could easily bruise
any leering teenage boy
who'd dare enter their realm,

so strongly do they stare
from the cheap book covers,
some so bold they'd never
cower or shudder,
potent, chiseled champions,
bodies tight as tension wire.

Talking to Marilyn

The psychics who are trying to bring you back
don't want to see that version of you
from *The Misfits,* they don't want to see you,

loveworn and hurt, clinging to the arms of a Gable
too far from being Rhett Butler. Neither do they
want the shy Norma Jean calendar pinup

whose hair had no trace of dye, face
fresh-scrubbed and nearly bare of makeup,
cheeks flushed with youth's inexperience.

The ladies round the ouija board tonight
only want to speak with the glam Marilyn,
the spike-heeled, fingernail-painted Marilyn—

pouty red lips, hair teased to a high halo
of blond iridescence. They want the Marilyn
who stood over the subway grate, white dress

billowing up while the train rumbled beneath,
the Marilyn who teetered to walk
past Tony Curtis and Jack Lemmon,

their jaws dropping on seeing her wiggle,
the Marilyn who cooed "Diamonds Are a Girl's
Best Friend," bejeweled and flirty,

sassy dress wrapped snug
around those Hollywood curves.
The psychics here tonight want

star power, their hands uniting to move
across the board one letter at a time,
trying to channel you back to an age

where your imitators are far too many
and far too untalented, girls
with bad manners and worse taste,

crass opportunists like Madonna, Sharon Stone.
They want your voice, breathy with confidence,
to come into this room, telling them you

never really meant to die, you had
more movies to make, more photos to shoot,
more glamor. *Come back to us,* they chant,

Let us hear you speak, say Madame Gina,
Mistress Clarice, and the magnificent Mrs. Amma,
my Aunt Magdalena leading them all,

her eyes shut, her wise mind full
of spiritual advice. But Marilyn doesn't
want to surface tonight—*her spirit's*

too tired, Madame Gina explains,
pulling her shawl over bony shoulders.
All she can tell us is no, Magdalena reveals,

disappointment creasing her face.
They regret letting me watch, I know it,
so I leave that storefront séance

quietly, taking my doubt with me,
my only chance to find out what becomes
a legend most ruined by a skepticism

strong as the harsh glaring light
that hits whenever I leave a movie's dark comfort,
trying to make sense of day.

Screen Test

*They don't make movies
like this anymore,* Mother would say
in delight, smiling as another
late-night movie filled
the television screen,
a splashy Esther Williams musical
replete with floating chorus girls
suspended in garish blue water.
Dismissing today's actors
with a wave of her hand,
she'd purse her lips in disgust
over Eddie Murphy's Beverly Hills
antics, Sly Stallone's gun-toting
machismo. *I wouldn't lose
a moment's sleep to watch
any of them,* she'd say, but
would stay up all night
to watch actors whose names
she made sure I knew:
tough guys Raft and Cagney
stalking gangland territory,
proud cowboys Alan Ladd and Randolph Scott
poised for sharpshooting, romantic leads
brooding in tight close-ups—Olivier
and Oberon pacing the desolate moors,
Robert Taylor and Greta Garbo
cinching passion in *Camille*.
And the musicals, with their
flimsy plots and hokey dialogue,

didn't escape her attention either—
Judy and Mickey hoofing it
on endless soundstages,
Rogers and Astaire bickering
everywhere but the dance floor,
or the sexy limbs of Cyd Charisse
flashing stealthily past.

But Mother never mentioned
the luminous beauty of Dorothy
Dandridge, the fine brown frame
of the young Ethel Waters,
or the café-au-lait charm
of matinee idol Lorenzo Tucker,
never commented on Robeson's
stoic strength. Never did she
detail the ugly parody
of blackface, so I was stunned
to find photos of stars from
Judy and Mickey to Shirley Temple
with monstrous, darkened faces.
Mother only seemed to know
the lovely Lena Horne,
who'd appear briefly in white films,
draped in nightclub satin to
sing one number, then disappear.
Only later did I learn
that movie theaters in the South
would snip out Lena's scenes,

her beige beauty offensive
to audiences accustomed
to the catty ways and ploys
of a chain-smoking Bette Davis.

Mother, I am learning now
for us both, captivated
as you surely would have been
had the late-night movie
had some color to it,
other than maids, cooks, fools.
You would have been thrilled
to see splendid Hazel Scott
caressing piano keys,
jazzing the classics with
skilled brown hands,
dynamic Katherine Dunham
dancing fervent on strong legs,
leading her troupe in authentic
African dance, vampy Nina Mae McKinney
seductive and quick as temptation
in an all-singing, all-dancing
all-black musical called *Hallelujah*.
We could have watched together,
seen faces like ours
illuminated on screen
for the whole world to watch.

Higher Education

Some people here look at me
as if I'm not actually a person,
but a walking statistic instead,
one of those aliens admitted
to keep the quotas up,
liberals happy.

They turn their heads
when they see me on line
at the college cafeteria,
fearing another one just like me
will be admitted soon, upsetting
delicate tradition. But some people

want to know all about me:
what those funny little braids I wear
are called, whether or not I know
the only black person in New York
they know, whether or not a white person
could walk safely in my neighborhood.

Others ask why blacks need a whole month
devoted to their history, and still others
want to know what my plan is
for saving America's inner cities.
One girl raised her hand in Sociology,
said, *I'm not prejudiced, but*

*why do all their neighborhoods
smell so bad?,* looking at me,
expecting an answer. Well, she
never got one, but her best friend
saw fit to explain later: *she just
doesn't know, you know, she's clueless.*

I came to this school to learn,
to find out what I wanted to know
and then begin from there, but
I find myself teaching, educating,
explaining why my hair is different,
why I feel no need to sunbathe,

why it's possible for me to love
both Aretha Franklin and Kate Bush,
Janis Joplin and Billie Holiday.
I'm learning more patience
than I'd ever thought I'd need,
equipped to deal with men

who ask *what's it like to be
a token?,* assuming that's the only way
I could get to sit in these hallowed
classrooms, the only way I could sleep
in these treasured dormitories
where the fathers of these boys

once slept, the rooms handed down
from one generation to the next.
When one of them asks, *don't
you think you'd be better off
at a school where there are more
people like you,* I wince,

but don't cry, I smile to cover
my sigh, say *more people like me
know just how to take care of people
like you,* my brown hand stroking
his white shoulder, making certain
he flinches, sure that he squirms.

Academic Instructions

Don't write
about being black.
All that racial jive

is passé anyway;
no one wants to hear
how waitresses won't

serve you, how plainclothes
detectives follow you
in up-scale shops, fearing

you'll shatter or steal
one-of-a-kind china and crystal,
afraid you'll send property values

plummeting by stepping through
their revolving doors. And please,
no more poems on being a woman,

we get far too many of those,
and frankly, they bore us,
sullen tales of first menses

and lost virginity,
smug complaints about male
appetites, detailed renderings

of all those body parts
that should stay hidden,
instead of peering

from blouses, peeking
from parted legs.
And don't, for heaven's sake,

say a word about being both,
it's been done and we're tired
of it, tired of your constant

ancestor worship—your love
of strong brown women,
mothers who tilled fields

and birthed babies,
clothed and fed and loved
the sick, insane, and poor,

who made churchgoing clothes
from some rich lady's scraps.
No one wants to hear

what you call your history;
its naive and mundane,
full of scandalous blame

for everyone but yourself.
Come back when you are ready
to learn how to write

like the rest of us,
when you're ready to admit
all the beauty in the world

around you, finally wise enough
to know nothing you say clearly
can ever matter.

The First Time

Old wives' tales didn't help,
locker room advice didn't prepare me
to be both broken and whole,

molten and arid, each cell in my body
not knowing whether to weep
or celebrate, whether to pull you in,

push you away? Was this the sort of peril
women were meant for, this inexplicable
danger? Eyes closed, I can go back

to that single precarious moment
where you separated me from myself, broke
the passage open, pushing past my ache,

past the gasp that rose from me
when you entered, making room,
settling in as if you belonged.

Afraid to move, afraid not
to move, I wanted distractions—
your mouth on mine, your hands

on my breasts. But you thrust deeper,
held my back tight in both hands
as we rocked in pain and sweetness,

and I felt old, older as I realized
there was no easy satisfaction
in this, no simple union

or sudden comfort, only greater questions,
only a bond we made looser each time
we sunk to our knees, every time I let you in.

The White People Next Door

have children who cannot hide
their curiosity. Each time

my husband and I step out the door,
they're there, in the way,

two small heads bobbing, eyes wide,
curly hair and straight hair,

two brothers, each no older than
five, who find it necessary

to ask every question they
can think of, wanting to know

where we're going, what we're
doing, will we be coming back?

Are you two married?, they ask,
high-pitched voices full of disbelief,

boy-faces puzzled as they try to grasp
how we could be married when I'm black

and my husband's white, that combination
wholly new to them, so foreign

they stutter as they ask about it,
mystified. Confused, they persist,

insisting I show them my baby,
a child I don't have, a fact

they refuse to accept, unable
to imagine how two adults could live

their lives without roller skates
on the sidewalk, tricycles

in the backyard. Smiling,
I tell them we don't have children,

and I walk away, remembering
how their father's voice

came through the wall that morning,
as it does so many mornings—*how many times*

do I have to tell you not to waste
my money? I paid good money for

this soap, and here you spray it
all over the damn bathroom!

Clean this mess up now before I
really hurt you! Don't you ever

do this again, or you'll really
be crying then! His tirades wake us

before we want to be awake, spurts
of hate that subside by the time

he leaves at eight. No wonder
those children are always

playing in our front yard,
yelling for us to watch them

on their roller skates,
their tricycles. No wonder

they want to know what our lives
are like, what we do, what we

eat. They want to know what it's like
to come and go in silence, to wake

without hearing their father
slamming through the bedrooms,

cursing their names. They want to know
just what goes on inside our apartment,

a place they can only see in glimpses
before we close the door behind us,

latching the locks, closing the drapes,
keeping our peace to ourselves.

Express Lane

Gimme my money, the young boy shouts,
but his grandmother's wise enough

to ignore him, blunting protest
with a shrug, a denial. They're

both behind me in the eight-
items-or-less lane, buying

something useful or needed before
the grocery's doors seal closed,

its cash registers clanging shut.
The woman's face is wrinkled,

brown, not kind, and she
has no sweet words when this

young boy repeats *stupid, I'm a
stupid boy,* his voice blatant, singsong.

She doesn't whisper to quiet him,
doesn't tell him he's loved,

doesn't put her gnarled hand
over his. Maybe she's given up

early, conceding that the world
won't value this boy as he

grows to be a man, wanting only
to jail him, confine him

to a prison cell's stripped space.
When the boy squeals for money

again, she says *it ain't your money,*
and the tone in her voice

lets him know it will never be
his money, the world closing up

and shrinking away for them both,
but especially for him, its aisles

unwelcoming, its commerce
intended for someone else.

Aftermath

After that first time
you had to coax me
back into your arms,

touching me softly,
not swiftly, reassuring
that we'd make it better,

that I wouldn't ache
every time, that joy
would eventually overtake

pain. We'd know
each other so intimately
there'd be no hesitations,

no afterthoughts, only
sensation and counter-
sensation, action and

reaction, my hands
skimming your curves,
your mouth roaming,

kissing the flesh that winds
back into itself, deep
into me. You told me

not to hide, not to hold
back, but to flow
into you, allowing

the great shifts to come
and come, feeling power
in our strength and heat,

all elements in motion,
a chemistry that keeps
reinventing us,

changing our mortal bodies
to beings we wouldn't know,
the transformation that stunning.

So I peeled everything
off, let my limbs loosen, open,
ready to receive you, to believe

we could remake our world
by doing what our bodies
told us to do—coming together

during the brightest part
of day—not the darkest—
everything visible, everything rising.

Plenty

I'm all lost in Fabric World,
the one-stop sewing supermarket
tucked in a strip mall on the
edge of town, a lonely string
of abandoned storefronts

where nothing thrives except
this lavish emporium dedicated
to needle and thread, to zippers
in all possible lengths.
Here I find patterns,

file cabinets packed with them;
I admire laces and trims,
those small decorative touches;
skim pattern catalogs complete
with color photos—all the dresses,

skirts, pants, and blouses
that anyone could sew, long as
they bought the right pattern,
right cloth. Cloth
surrounds me everywhere here,

wrapped on heavy bolts, ready
to be touched, cut. Loving
the textures I find, I walk
from aisle to aisle, whispering
fabric names: cotton, linen,

silk and wool, crepe, flannel,
fleece and gabardine, brocade,
chiffon, satin and tweed,
corduroy, denim, poplin
and seersucker. Here I find

voile, so lightweight and sheer
that I don't dare touch it;
I find velvet so lush I can't resist
letting one finger trail through
its plush nap; taffeta for airy blouses,

skimpy dresses; broadcloth tightly woven
and strong. Here are the glittery metallics
that glide off the bolt like liquid metal;
here's the fake fur, and yes, even
the double knit's here, that ill-fated

acrylic. And the designs overwhelm me:
boastful strident plaids,
tricky stripes and diagonals,
polka dots, country calico,
floral motifs, African prints.

So much for my eyes to take in—
moody midnight blues,
sensual apple reds, rich browns
the same shade as a perfectly aged
Stradivarius. Who cares that I

can't sew, that I don't have
a sewing machine to call my own,
that I have trouble seeing the eye
of almost every needle. I am here
because I love to think

of all the things that can be made
from these yards and yards of cloth,
the combinations infinite as long
as the shears are sharp, pincushions full,
threads pulled tight in every seam.

ACKNOWLEDGMENTS

Many thanks to the following magazines and periodicals, where some of the poems in this book have appeared: *Callaloo* ("Artist-in-Residence," "It's Tough to Be a Girl Scout in the City," "On Sidewalks, on Street Corners, as Girls," "Playing Rough," "Plenty," "Señora Williams,""Summers on Screvin," and "The Tenant"); *Kenyon Review* ("Barbie's Little Sister" and "My Father's Heroes"); *Many Mountains Moving* ("Traitor"); and *Tomorrow Magazine* ("Bribery").

I also wish to thank the following people for their help and support: Carolyn Alessio, Beth Lordan, Rodney Jones, Maura Stanton, and Jon Tribble.

Thanks also to the Illinois Arts Council for a 1995–1996 Fellowship in Poetry.

 ALLISON JOSEPH is the author of two previous collections of poetry: *What Keeps Us Here* (1992) and *Soul Train* (1997). *What Keeps Us Here* was the first winner of the Ampersand Press Women Poets Series Competition and was also awarded the 1992 John C. Zacharis Prize from Emerson College and *Ploughshares*. Joseph lives in Carbondale, Illinois, where she teaches at Southern Illinois University.

Library of Congress Cataloging-in-Publication Data

Joseph, Allison, 1967–
　　In every seam / Allison Joseph.
　　　　　p.　　cm. — (Pitt poetry series)
　　ISBN 0-8229-3994-0 (alk. paper). — ISBN 0-8229-5641-1
(pbk : alk. paper)
　　I. Title. II. Series.
PS 3560.0772315　1997
811'.54—dc21　　　96-45880